Nelson
Grammar

Pupil Book 2

OXFORD
UNIVERSITY PRESS

OXFORD
UNIVERSITY PRESS

Great Clarendon Street, Oxford, OX2 6DP, United Kingdom

Oxford University Press is a department of the University of Oxford.
It furthers the University's objective of excellence in research, scholarship,
and education by publishing worldwide. Oxford is a registered trade mark
of Oxford University Press in the UK and in certain other countries

Text © Wendy Wren 2014
Illustrations © Céline Deregnaucourt, Bethan Matthews,
Maggie Morales and Simon Smith 2014

The moral rights of the author have been asserted

First published 2014

British Library Cataloguing in Publication Data

Data available

ISBN: 978-1-4085-2389-6

3 5 7 9 10 8 6 4

Paper used in the production of this book is a natural, recyclable product made from
wood grown in sustainable forests. The manufacturing process conforms to the
environmental regulations of the country of origin.

Printed in China by Imago

Acknowledgements

Series editor: John Jackman
Cover illustration: Marcus Cutler
Page make-up: OKS Prepress, India

Oxford OWL
Discover eBooks, inspirational
resources, advice and support
www.oxfordowl.co.uk

Contents

Book 2 Scope and Sequence

Unit	Pupil Book Focus	Pupil Book Practice	Pupil Book Extension	Workbook Support	Workbook Extension	Resource Book Support	Resource Book Extension
1	**nouns & adjectives**: pairing nouns & adjectives, noun phrase	descriptive sentence writing based on picture stimulus	improving a passage by adding appropriate adjectives	identifying nouns & adjectives/supplying nouns & adjectives in a given context	descriptive sentence writing based on picture stimulus & vocabulary box	Identifying nouns in sentences/completing sentences with appropriate adjectives from picture stimulus	listing nouns/ supplying adjectives to describe picture/ descriptive writing about themselves
2	**adjectives**: opposites*	making sentences opposite by changing adjectives	adjective opposites with prefix *un*/writing sentences	identifying adjectives in sentences/making sentences opposites	making adjectives opposite with *un*/completing sentences with adjectives	labeling pictures with appropriate adjectives/match the opposites	using adjectives in sentence writing
3	**nouns**: collective*	defining collective nouns	one collective noun – two groups/writing sentences	writing appropriate collective nouns/ completing sentences with collective nouns	collective noun crossword/ defining unusual collective nouns	choosing appropriate collective nouns/ sorting muddled collective nouns	noun – verb agreement with collective nouns
4	**verbs**: present progressive tense	identifying verbs/ forming present progressive verbs	completing sentences with verbs	choosing *am*, *is* or *are*/completing verb webs	sentence writing from picture stimulus	identifying present progressive verbs/ word sums	writing present tense verbs for picture clues/ sentence writing
5	**nouns**: proper nouns – places	writing proper nouns with capital letters/ identifying proper nouns	completing sentences with proper nouns	identifying proper nouns/writing place names/correcting sentences with missing capital letters	sentence writing from picture stimulus	writing the days of the week/writing place names for map	completing A, B, C... list of proper nouns
6	**sentences**: making sense	ordering words to make sentences	completing sentences	sentence writing from picture stimulus	writing sentences for narrative sequence	adding capital letters & full stops to sentences	identifying sentences/ correcting non-sentences
7	**contractions**: apostrophes – present tense verb *to be*	writing words that make contractions/ writing contractions	matching pairs of words to contractions	identifying contractions/ writing contractions	writing contractions in speech	writing contractions/ writing contractions in speech	contractions/ adding missing apostrophes to text
8	**conjunctions**: *and* & *but*	joining sentences with *and* & *but*	choosing appropriate conjunction	choosing appropriate conjunctions/joining sentences	identifying sentences that have been joined/ joining sentences	identifying conjunctions/joining sentences	writing sentences from picture stimulus
9	**adverbs**: manner	completing sentences with given adverbs	completing sentences with own adverbs	matching verbs & adverbs/using pairs in sentences	word sums – forming adverbs from adjectives ending in *y*/ writing sentences	words sums – forming adverbs from adjectives/identifying appropriate adverbs/ writing sentences	answering questions with adverbs/building sentences with adverbs and adjectives
10	**verbs**: regular past simple tense	completing sentences with regular past simple tense verbs	words sums – infinitives ending in *consonant + y* & *vowel + y*	identifying regular past simple tense verbs/ writing sentences	forming regular past simple tense verbs/changing present tense sentences to past tense	completing sentences/ completing verb table	forming regular past simple tense verbs/using them in sentences
11	**nouns**: compound	joining nouns to make compound nouns	identifying compound nouns in continuous prose/writing sentences	writing compound nouns from picture stimuli/forming compound nouns from lists	forming multiple compound nouns with the same root.	writing compound nouns from picture clues	writing groups of compound noun with same beginnings
12	**sentences**: statements/questions/ exclamations/ commands	identifying & punctuating statements/ questions/ exclamations	changing statements into questions/ identifying commands	identifying & punctuating statements/ questions/ exclamations	writing questions with given question words/ punctuating sentences	identifying statements/questions/ exclamations/writing questions	writing questions to match answers
13	**pronouns**: personal*	substituting pronouns for nouns in sentences/writing sentences	writing sentences with pronouns based on picture stimulus	identifying pronouns/ completing sentences with pronouns	replacing nouns with pronouns in sentences/ identifying use of pronouns	matching pronouns & pictures/replacing nouns with pronouns in sentences	using pronouns to avoid repetition in sentences/ completing sentences
14	**contractions**: apostrophes – present tense of the verb *to have*	making pronoun + verb into contractions/using contractions in sentences	making noun + verb into contractions	identifying contractions/ forming contractions	differentiating between same contractions for verbs *to be* & *to have*	writing contractions in speech	forming contractions & using in sentences
15	**commas**: lists in sentences	adding missing commas	constructing sentences from given vocabulary	adding missing conjunction & commas	constructing sentences from given vocabulary/ writing sentences	adding missing conjunctions/adding missing commas	constructing sentences from given vocabulary/ writing sentences

*denotes content that is not specified in the National Curriculum for England (2014) but which will support children's wider knowledge and understanding of grammar.

Unit	Pupil Book Focus	Pupil Book Practice	Pupil Book Extension	Workbook Support	Workbook Extension	Resource Book Support	Resource Book Extension
16	**adjectives:** comparatives with *er*	completing sentences with comparative adjectives	sorting adjectives & comparative adjectives	identifying adjectives & comparative adjectives in sentences/ completing table	forming comparative adjectives from adjectives ending in *e* & *y*	writing comparative adjectives/writing sentences	forming comparative adjectives/using in sentences
17	**nouns:** possessive – singular	adding apostrophe to owner in sentences	shortening sentences using possessive nouns/writing sentences	writing phrases using apostrophe/ identifying the owner/ adding missing apostrophes	Adding missing apostrophes/ writing sentences with apostrophe of possession	identifying possessive nouns in sentences/ adding apostrophes/ shortening phrases with possessive nouns	shortening phrases with possessive nouns/sentence writing
18	**contractions:** contractions with *not*; apostrophes	completing sentences with contractions	identifying & writing contractions	matching word pairs & contractions/ writing sentences	writing contractions/ using in sentences	identifying contractions in sentences/writing contractions	writing contractions in speech
19	**verbs:** past progressive tense	changing verbs from present simple to past progressive	completing sentences with past progressive verbs	identifying past progressive verbs in sentences/ completing verb table	completing sentences with past progressive verbs/writing sentences with past simple and past progressive tense verbs	completing verb table/ writing sentences	changing sentences from past simple to past progressive/ present simple to past progressive
20	**adjectives:** superlative with *est*	completing sentences with superlative adjectives	sorting adjectives - comparatives & superlatives	identifying adjectives and superlatives/ completing adjective table	completing adjective table with adjectives that need doubling/ending in *y* & *e*	forming superlative adjectives/writing sentences	forming superlative adjectives/using in sentence writing/ comparing two & three things
21	**adverbs:** when & where	sorting adverbs	answering questions using adverbs/ completing sentences with adverbs	identifying adverbs in sentences/ completing sentences with adverbs	expanding sentences with adverbs/choosing adverbs and using in sentences	adverb word sums/ sorting adverbs/ writing sentences	forming adverbs from adjectives ending in *ible* and *able*/writing sentences
22	**verbs:** past progressive tense	identifying the continuous action in sentences	changing statements to questions	identifying past simple and past progressive tense verbs/completing sentences with past progressive tense verbs	writing sentences containing a past simple and a past progressive tense verb	matching past simple & past progressive tense verbs/writing sentences	completing sentences/changing statements into questions
23	**conjunctions:** *and/but/or*	joining with *and/ but/or*	joining with *but* & *or*/ using pronouns	joining with *and, but* or *or*	writing short sentences and joining from picture stimulus	identifying short sentences/writing sentences with given conjunctions	joining with *and, but* or *or* /using pronouns
24	**confusing words:** *to/two/too; there/their/ they're; were/where/ we're**	completing sentences	completing sentences/ writing sentences	completing sentences/ writing sentences with all three words	completing sentences with *there, their* & *they're*/writing sentence with all three words	completing sentences/ writing sentences	completing sentences with *were, where* &*we're*/writing sentence with all three words
25	**conjunctions:** *so/ because/and/but*	joining sentences using pronouns	joining sentences using *when/if/that*	identifying conjunctions/ joining sentences	joining sentences/ using pronouns/ writing sentences with given conjunctions	identifying short sentences/writing sentences with given conjunctions	joining sentences/ using pronouns
26	**adverbs:** comparative & superlative adverbs*	completing sentences with given adverbs	sorting comparative & superlative adverbs	completing adverb table/identifying adverbs/writing sentences with given adverbs	completing sentences with irregular comparatives & superlatives/ identifying adjective or adverb in context	completing sentences/ writing sentences	writing sentences with given irregular adverbs
27	**nouns:** formed with suffixes	adding suffixes *er* & *ing*	expanding sentences with *ness, er* & *ing*	forming nouns from verb with *er* & *ing*	forming nouns with *ness* from adjectives ending in *y*/writing sentences	completing sentences with *ness* nouns/ writing sentences	matching adjective and noun/writing sentences
28	**adjectives:** formed with suffixes	solving clues with *ful* & *less* adjectives/ completing phrases	completing sentences with *ful* & *less* adjectives	forming adjectives/ writing sentences with given adjectives	forming adjectives with *ful* & *less* from nouns ending in *y*	forming adjective opposites	writing sentences with given adjectives

Nouns and adjectives

Nouns are **naming** words.

snail

flame

'A snail' and 'the flame' are **noun phrases**.

Adjectives are **describing** words.

They tell us more about a person, animal or thing.

small   dirty   happy

white   old   big

Focus

Write the *noun* for each picture.

Choose an *adjective* from the box for each noun.

little	fluffy	brown	big	long	fat

1 _____

2 _____

3 _____

4 _____

5 _____

6 _____

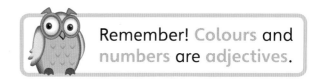

Remember! Colours and numbers are adjectives.

Look at the picture.

Write some sentences to *describe* the picture.

Extension

This story has no *adjectives*.

Copy the story into your book.

Add *adjectives* to make it more interesting.

The farmer was working in the field. He was wearing a coat, scarf and a hat. On his feet he wore boots. He drove the tractor up and down the fields. He will plant seeds. The seeds will grow into corn.

Adjectives

Adjectives are describing words.

a big elephant

a long snake

Adjectives have opposites.

a little mouse

a short worm

Read each *adjective* in Box 1.

Find the *opposite* in Box 2.

Box 1	Box 2
bright	bent
strong	dirty
straight	dull
hard	blunt
sharp	soft
clean	weak

Copy the sentences.

Replace each coloured *adjective* with its *opposite* from the box.

loose	new	quiet	warm	dry

1 It is a cold day.

2 There was a loud knock.

3 I have wet hair!

4 This is a very tight knot.

5 Look at this old book.

Some *adjectives* make their opposites with *un*.

happy　　　unhappy　　　kind　　　unkind

A What are the *opposites* of these adjectives?

　1 wise　　　**2** well　　　**3** true　　　**4** lucky

B Use each *opposite* you have made in a sentence of your own.

Nouns

A **noun** is the name of a person, animal, place or thing.

A **collective noun** is a special name for a **group of nouns**.

a **swarm** of bees

a **fleet** of ships

Focus

Choose a word from the box to go with each *collective noun*.

books	*wolves*	*flowers*
trees	*sheep*	*cows*

1 a forest of _____

2 a herd of _____

3 a bunch of _____

4 a flock of _____

5 a pack of _____

6 a library of _____

What would you expect to find in each of these groups?

1 an army

2 a crew

3 a pride

4 an orchestra

5 a bouquet

6 a gaggle

Extension

A Sometimes we use the same collective noun for two different groups.

Find two things for each collective noun.

1 *a pack of* _____ and _____
2 *a herd of* _____ and _____
3 *a bunch of* _____ and _____
4 *a flock of* _____ and _____

B Choose three collective nouns from A.

Use each collective noun in a sentence of your own.

Verbs

Verbs are doing words.
Verbs tell us what people are doing.

| He is singing. | She is reading. | It is running. | They are riding. |

Focus

Choose a *verb* from the box to go with each picture.

| is jumping | are drinking | is kicking |
| are swimming | is writing | is sleeping |

1 She _____ . **2** He _____ . **3** They _____ .

4 They _____ . **5** It _____ . **6** It _____ .

A Write the *verb* in each sentence.

   1 The ship is sailing on the sea.

   2 The clock is ticking loudly.

   3 The wind is blowing the leaves about.

   4 I am reading my book.

   5 They are playing a game.

B Write the *present tense verbs*.

   1 hop   She is hopping.

   2 smile   We __ _____.

   3 clap   They __ _____.

   4 wave   I __ _____.

   5 bake   She __ _____.

The first one is done for you.

Copy the sentences.

Choose a *verb* of your own to fill each gap.

1 I ____ _____ sand castles on the beach.

2 The snow ____ _____ very quickly.

3 He ____ _____ his bicycle.

4 We ____ _____outside in the summer.

5 The dog ____ _____ the cat.

Nouns

Nouns are naming words.

hen   bicycle   table

Proper nouns are special naming words.

They have **capital letters**.

Names of people are special naming words.   Mrs Hill

Days of the week are special naming words.   Monday

Months of the year are special naming words.   January

The **names of places** are special naming words. Midtown

Focus

A Write these headings in your book.

nouns	proper nouns

B Write each *noun* from the box under the correct heading.

boot   Naseem   cart   Ben
Mr Evans   bowl   Mrs Patel
horse   fish   Harry   London
girl   Africa   milk   Amy

A Write these *proper nouns* correctly.

1 mrs Kelly   **2** africa   **3** tuesday

4 sam   **5** april   **6** doctor jones

7 sheila   **8** america   **9** mr black

B Look at the words in the box.

Find the proper nouns. Write them correctly.

hat	fred	kim	tree	monday	meg
book	dog	car	england	cat	cardiff

Extension

Copy these sentences.

Use a *proper noun* to finish each sentence.

1 My name is _____.

2 My friend's name is _____.

3 My birthday is in _____.

4 The first day of the week is _____.

5 The country I live in is _____.

Sentences

A **sentence**:

- begins with a **capital letter**.
- ends with a **full stop**, a **question mark** or an **exclamation mark**.
- makes **sense**.

Full stops, question marks and exclamation marks are all types of punctuation.

This is a **sentence**:

 The clouds in the sky are grey.

This is **NOT** a sentence:

 in the sky

Focus

A Which of these are *sentences*?

 1 The bus was late.

 2 the broken glass was

 3 it rained all day

 4 in the sun

 5 In winter it is very cold.

 6 I am going to

B Copy the sentences from A.

Remember! Sentences make **sense**.

Remember how to begin and end a sentence.

Look for the capital letter and full stop.

Write the words in the correct order to make *sentences*.

1 has   cake   eight   The   candles.   birthday

2 are   the   There   in   flowers   vase.

3 The   on   table.   was   the   food

Extension

Fill the gaps to make each of these a *sentence*.

| After | two | cats | Flowers | Today |

1 _____ grow in the spring.

Use the words in the box or your own ideas.

2 Dogs like to chase _____ .

3 _____ tea, we went out to play.

4 Bicycles have _____ wheels.

5 _____ is my birthday.

Contractions

If something contracts it gets smaller.

Contractions are words that get smaller.

- A letter or letters are missed out.
- An apostrophe goes in place of the missing letter or letters.

   This is an apostrophe.

I am looking for my gloves. I'm looking for my gloves.

I am	=	I'm	a is missed out
you are	=	you're	a is missed out
he is	=	he's	i is missed out
she is	=	she's	i is missed out
it is	=	it's	i is missed out
we are	=	we're	a is missed out
you are	=	you're	a is missed out
they are	=	they're	a is missed out

Focus

Copy the lists.

Match the *contractions*.

The first one has been done for you.

we are   he's

you are   they're

he is   she's

it is   we're

they are   it's

she is   you're

A Write the words that make these *contractions*.

1 she's   2 they're   3 we're

4 it's   5 you're   6 I'm

B Copy the sentences.

Write the coloured words as *contractions*.

1 I am not happy.

2 She is late.

3 He is lost!

4 We are eating.

5 They are at home.

Match the *contractions* in the box to words in the list.

1 I will

2 we have

3 cannot

4 I have

5 she had

6 do not

7 would not

8 let us

9 did not

10 who is

There are lots of other contractions.

I've

she'd

I'll

we've

wouldn't

didn't

who's

don't

can't

let's

Conjunctions

Conjunctions are joining words.
We use them to **join** sentences.

Give me the bag. I will unpack it.
Give me the bag **and** I will unpack it.

The telephone rang. No one answered it.
The telephone rang **but** no one answered it.

Focus

Read the sentences.
Say the *conjunction* in each sentence.

1 Fred did not sleep but he was not tired the next day.

2 Sarah likes oranges and she likes apples.

3 The birds made a nest but they did not lay any eggs.

4 We got there on time but we missed the train.

5 We played well and won the match.

A Copy the sentences. Join each pair with *and*.

1 Go to the shops.
Buy some bread.

2 I found my book.
I finished it.

3 I ran quickly.
I caught the bus.

B Copy the sentences. Join each pair with *but*.

1 The car crashed.
The driver was not hurt.

2 I want a plum.
There are none left.

3 I like to swim.
I'm not very good.

Use *and* or *but* to join these sentences.

1 I have lost my pencil. I need it.

2 Max forgot his lunch. He was very hungry.

3 It was very cold. My new coat kept me warm.

4 She likes drawing. She does not like painting.

5 Take this box. Leave the other one.

Adverbs

An adverb tells us more about how something is done.

> Adverb = adds to a verb

The boy is shouting.

The boy is shouting loudly.

> verb   adverb

The lightning flashes.

The lightning flashes brightly.

> verb   adverb

Many adverbs are made like this:

adjective	+	ly	adverb
loud	+	ly	loudly
bright	+	ly	brightly

Focus

Do the word sums. Say the *adverbs*.

1 quiet + ly =   2 slow + ly =

3 quick + ly =   4 neat + ly =

5 calm + ly =   6 honest + ly =

7 kind + ly =   8 sad + ly =

Complete the sentences with *adverbs* from the box.

> loudly   strongly   quickly   fiercely   neatly

1 Harry ran _____ to catch the bus.

2 The band played _____ so everyone could hear.

3 Sara wrote her story _____.

4 The wind blew _____ and scattered the leaves.

5 The lion roared _____.

Copy and complete the sentences with *adverbs* of your own.
1 The boy is singing _____.
2 The boy is shouting _____.
3 The boy is laughing _____.
4 The boy is waving _____.
5 The boy is sleeping _____.

Verbs

Verbs are doing words.

Past tense verbs tell us what people, animals and things did.

- verb family name + ed

    gallop + ed galloped

- verb family name ending in e + d

    smile + d smiled

Focus

A Write these headings in your book.

+ ed	+ d

B Read the *verb family names* in the box.

wave	talk	clean	chase	smile	wash
skate	dive	brush	look	bake	watch
move	cook	push	scratch	like	save

C Write the *past tense verb* under the correct heading.

Complete these sentences with a *past tense verb*.

1 Mum _____ a cake for my birthday.

2 We _____ a good film on TV.

3 I _____ my teeth before I went to bed.

4 I _____ the house for pocket money.

5 He _____ into the pool.

- Verbs ending in vowel + y, just added ed.

    play = play**ed**

- Verbs ending in consonant + y, change y to i and add ed.

    hurry = hurr**ied**

Do these word sums. Write the *past tense verbs*.

1 enjoy + ed =   **2** copy + ed =

3 study + ed =   **4** sway + ed =

5 obey + ed =   **6** bury + ed =

Nouns

There are many different types of nouns.

Common nouns tell us the names of ordinary things.

watch   table   box

Proper nouns are:

- people's names   Mr Price
- days and months   Monday   April
- places   London   Scotland

Collective nouns tell us the names of groups of things.

flock of sheep   bunch of grapes

Another type of noun is a compound noun.

We make compound nouns by joining two
nouns together.

table + cloth = tablecloth

Focus

Write the *compound nouns* for each of these.

1   2   3

4   5   6

A Match each noun from the first box with a noun from the second box to make a *compound noun*.

space
egg
rain
neck
door
book

lace
ship
cup
coat
mark
step

B Use two of the *compound nouns* you have made in sentences of your own.

Extension

A Make a list of the *compound nouns* in this passage.

It was the day of an important football match. Sally was excited because she was the goalkeeper. She was so excited that she forgot to do her homework and her schoolteacher was not pleased. At twelve o'clock the team went out. They walked along the footpath to get to the pitch. Sally put her tracksuit by the goalpost and waited for the match to begin.

B Use these *compound nouns* in sentences of your own.

1 flowerbed	**2** hillside	**3** daylight
4 housework	**5** waterfall	**6** stairway

Sentences

A **sentence** that starts with a **capital letter** and ends with a **full stop** is a **telling** sentence. It is a statement.

The duck is on the pond.

 This is a **statement**.

A sentence that starts with a **capital letter** and ends with a **question mark** is an **asking** sentence. It is a question.

Where is the duck?

This is a **question**.

A sentence that starts with a **capital letter** and ends with an **exclamation mark** shows people are:

shouting   angry   surprised

It is an **exclamation**.

Find the duck!

This is an **exclamation**. Some exclamations are **commands**.

Focus

Say which is:

- a *statement*   • a *question*   • an *exclamation*

1 I looked at the moon last night.

2 What time did you go to bed?

3 Did it snow last night?   4 I was very tired.

5 I went to bed so late!   6 I was late for school!

Copy the sentences. End each one with:

- a *full stop*
- a *question mark*   OR
- an *exclamation mark.*

1 Where are the shops

2 Is it time to go

3 I like drawing

4 Watch out

5 Do you like football

6 What a lovely surprise

Extension

A Make each one of these statements into *questions*.

1

It is raining.

2

You are ill.

3

They are late.

B

> A **command** tells you to do something.
>
>   Go to bed!
>
> Sometimes it has an exclamation mark, but not always.
>
>   Turn out the lights.

Which of these exclamations are also commands?

1 Tomorrow is sports day!   Bring your trainers!

2 Tidy your room!   What a mess!

Pronouns

A **pronoun** can be used instead of a **noun**.

The **girl** is running.

girl = **noun**

She is running.

She = **pronoun**

The **boy** is running.

boy = **noun**

He is running.

He = **pronoun**

These are **pronouns**.

I   you   he   she   it   we   they

Focus

Find the pronouns in these sentences.

Some sentences have more than one **pronoun**.

1 Where is he going?

2 He is going to the stream.

3 What has he found?

4 Where did he put it?

5 He has put it in a jar.

Practice

Copy the sentences.

Use *pronouns* instead of the coloured words.

1 The little girl has an ice cream.

2 The elephant has a long trunk.

3 Where are the boys playing?

4 Can you see the lion?

Extension

Look at the picture.

Write a sentence using a *pronoun* in each answer.

1 What is the boy doing?

2 What is the girl doing?

3 What is the cat doing?

4 What is the dog doing?

5 What are the birds doing?

Contractions

If something **contracts** it gets **smaller**.

Contractions are words that get smaller.

- A letter or letters are **missed out**.

- An **apostrophe** goes in place of the missing letter or letters.

This is an **apostrophe**.

I **have** lost my book.			I've lost my book.
I **have**	=	I've	ha is missed out
you **have**	=	you've	ha is missed out
he **has**	=	he's	ha is missed out
she **has**	=	she's	ha is missed out
it **has**	=	it's	ha is missed out
we **have**	=	we've	ha is missed out
you **have**	=	you've	ha is missed out
they **have**	=	they've	ha is missed out

Focus

Copy the lists.

Match the contractions.

The first one is done for you.

you have	he's
we have	they've
he has	she's
it has	you've
they have	it's
she has	we've

A Write the words that make these *contractions*.

1 she's   **2** they've   **3** we've

4 it's   **5** you've   **6** I've

B Copy the sentences.

Write the coloured words as contractions.

1 I have something to tell you.

2 She has forgotten her coat.

3 He has missed the bus!

4 You have done very well.

5 They have washed all the dishes.

Extension

We use contractions with pronouns.

   It's gone in the water

We use contractions with nouns.

   The ball's gone in the water.

Write the *contraction* for the underlined words.

1 The <u>train has</u> arrived on time.

2 <u>Sally has</u> made the tea.

3 <u>Tom has</u> seen it before.

4 The <u>tree has</u> lost its leaves.

5 My <u>aunt has</u> sent me a card.

Commas

When we write a list in a sentence we use commas.
We can join the last two things in the list with and.
This is a comma. **,**

   I am learning to add, take away, divide and multiply.

Focus

Say where the *commas* should go.

1 Nathan likes to read write and draw.

2 I like apples oranges bananas and plums.

3 We take books pencils and paper to school.

4 Cat dog book and girl are nouns.

5 We run jump skip and hop in the playground.

Copy the sentences.

Add the missing *commas*.

1 I live with my mother father sister and brother.

2 We have a table four chairs and a cooker in our kitchen.

3 Mum buys bread milk fruit and vegetables at the market.

Extension

Use the words in the box to write a sentence using *commas*.

1 Begin your sentence   At school we _____

| sing | read | write |

2 Begin your sentence   At the market we buy _____

| potatoes | cabbages | carrots |

Adjectives

Words like **bigger** and **smaller** are **comparative adjectives**.

Adjectives are **describing words**.
They tell us more about people, animals, places and things.

an **enormous** elephant   an **old** car

Adjectives can describe the **difference between two things**.

old man   **older** man   **small** bicycle   **smaller** bicycle

---

Focus

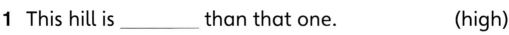

Read the sentences.

Add *er* to the adjective in brackets.

1 This hill is _____ than that one.   (high)

2 My hands are _____ than yours.   (clean)

3 My radio is _____ than yours.   (loud)

4 This bread is _____ than those rolls.   (fresh)

5 It is _____ today than it was yesterday.   (cold)

6 Is the river _____ than that pond?   (deep)

Copy the sentences.

Fill each gap with a *comparative adjective* from the box.

faster   higher   warmer   harder

1 I can jump _____ than you.

2 This new car goes _____ than the old one.

3 It was _____ to cycle up the hill than down the hill.

4 If the weather is _____ today we can wear shorts.

Write these headings.

adjective	comparative adjective

Write each word in the box under the correct heading.

cold   straight   thicker   softer   sharp   smooth
colder   straighter   great   thick   greater   soft
small   smoother   sharper   smaller

Nouns

Possessive nouns tell you who **owns** something.

They have an **apostrophe** and an **s** at the end.

Ruth's bicycle

Ruth is the **owner**.

This is a an apostrophe'.

Ruth's bicycle means the same as **the bicycle belonging to Ruth**.

Roger's book

Roger is the **owner**.

Roger's book means the same as **the book belonging to Roger**.

The **'s** tells you who or what the **owner** is.

Focus

Say who the *owner* is.

1 Deepak's football
2 the girl's laugh
3 the flower's stem
4 the doctor's coat
5 the dog's lead
6 the car's engine
7 Nigel's shoes
8 the farmer's field
9 the captain's ship
10 the boy's hair

Copy the sentences.

Add an *apostrophe* to the name of the *owner* in each sentence.

1 Garys homework was very hard.

2 Anji found the dogs lead in the park.

3 That mans tie has red and blue spots.

4 The cats claws were very sharp.

5 In the autumn, that trees leaves fall off.

6 The books cover was torn.

A Write each of these in a shorter way using a *possessive noun*.

1 The hand belonging to the girl.

2 The dinner belonging to the boy.

3 The tail belonging to the mouse.

4 The song belonging to the bird.

5 The wheels belonging to the tractor.

6 The paw belonging to the dog.

B Write six sentences of your own using a *possessive noun* from A in each one.

Contractions

If something **contracts** it gets **smaller**.

Contractions are words that are smaller.

- A letter or letters are **missed out**.
- An **apostrophe** goes in place of the missing letter or letters.

This is an **apostrophe**.

I am sorry.	**I'm** sorry.
I have lost my book.	**I've** lost my book.

> The **o** of not is missed out.

There are lots of **contractions** with **not**.

That **is not** right.	That **isn't** right.
They **have not** arrived.	They **haven't** arrived.

Focus

A Write the *contractions*.

1 is not **2** are not **3** must not

4 do not **5** does not **6** cannot

B Write the words that make these *contractions*.

1 wouldn't **2** haven't **3** hasn't

4 wasn't **5** weren't **6** shouldn't

Copy the sentences.

Write the coloured words as *contractions*.

1 He has not found his football.

2 They are not sure where it is.

3 It is not under the bush.

4 They have not looked behind
the shed.

5 We do not know where it is.

Write the *contraction* in each sentence.

Next to it, write the words it replaces.

1 "The ball's gone into the pond!" shouted Nelson.

2 "I'll need a long stick to get it out," said Luke.

3 "I'll go and look in the shed," said Nelson.

4 "Don't forget to bring a cloth," said Luke.

5 "We won't need a cloth," said Nelson.

6 "We'll have to dry the ball," said Luke.

Verbs

Verbs are doing words.

Past tense verbs tell us what people, animals and things did.

To make the past tense, we usually add ed or d to the verb family name.

This is the past simple tense.

I combed my hair.   I washed my face.
I walked to the door.   I picked up my bag.

Another way to make the past tense is like this:

This is the past progressive tense.

Past tense of the verb to be	+ verb family name	+ ing	
I was	sing	ing	I was singing.
You were	point	ing	You were pointing.
He was	help	ing	He was helping.
She was	laugh	ing	She was laughing.
It was	rain	ing	It was raining.
We were	jump	ing	We were jumping.
You were	shout	ing	You were shouting.
They were	fight	ing	They were fighting.

Focus

Read the sentences.

Which two words make up the *past progressive tense*?

1 The birds were flying around the garden.

2 The tree was bending in the wind.

3 The ducks were quacking for some food.

4 The dog was scattering leaves everywhere.

These sentences are in the present tense.
Change the underlined verb to the *past tense*.

1 I <u>am playing</u> with my dog.

2 You <u>are watching</u> television.

3 He <u>is reading</u> a book.

4 She <u>is washing</u> her hair.

5 It <u>is raining</u>.

6 We <u>are going</u> on holiday.

7 They <u>are visiting</u> the castle.

Extension

Each verb is made up of two words.

Copy and complete these sentences with *past tense verbs*.

1 I _____ _____ a snowman.

2 We _____ _____ when we saw the accident.

3 She _____ _____ to bed very late.

4 He _____ _____ breakfast when the post came.

Adjectives

Adjectives are **describing** words.

They tell us more about people, animals, places and things.

an **old** car

Words like **oldest** are **superlative** adjectives.

Adjectives can describe the **difference between two things**.

an **old** car

an **older** car

Adjectives can describe the difference between three or more things.

an **old** car

an **older** car

the **oldest** car

Focus

Read the sentences.

Add *est* to the adjective in brackets.

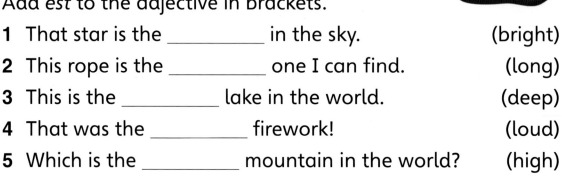

1 That star is the _____ in the sky.   (bright)

2 This rope is the _____ one I can find.   (long)

3 This is the _____ lake in the world.   (deep)

4 That was the _____ firework!   (loud)

5 Which is the _____ mountain in the world?   (high)

6 They are building the _____ building ever!   (tall)

Copy the sentences.
Fill each gap with a *superlative adjective* from the box.

> warmest   kindest   *freshest*   shortest

1 She is the _____ person I have ever met.

2 That's the _____ film I have ever seen!

3 This is the _____ day of the year.

4 I need the _____ vegetables you have.

Write these headings.

> adjective   comparative adjective   superlative adjective

Write each word in the box under the correct heading.

> quiet   newer   tighter   shortest   *full*   new
> *fuller*   tightest   short   quieter   tight   *fullest*
>   quietest   shorter   newest

Adverbs

An **adverb** tells us more about **how** something is done.

He walked **quickly**.   She read **slowly**.

Adverbs can also tell us **when** or **where** something is done.

When?   I saw my friend **yesterday**.

When did you **see** your friend?   Yesterday

I will tidy my room **later**.

When will you **tidy** your room?   Later

Where? I have put the books **here**.

Where have you **put** the books?   Here

I looked **everywhere** for the cat!

Where have you **looked** for the cat?   Everywhere

Focus

Find the *adverbs* in each sentence.

1 We put the cat outside when it is dark.

2 Sam carefully copied the sentences.

3 She always buys flowers at the market.

4 It rained heavily all day.

5 I get up early on a Saturday.

A Write these headings in your book.

how	when	where

B Write each *adverb* under the correct heading.

slowly	later	outside	here	angrily
never	sweetly	neatly	often	inside

Extension

A Write a sentence to answer each question. Use *adverbs*.

1 When will you do your homework?

2 Where do you catch the bus?

3 When can you come out to play?

4 How do you pack your schoolbag?

5 How do you eat your breakfast?

B Use *adverbs* to fill the gaps.

1 Please move _____ to your next lesson.

(how adverb)

2 You can tidy your books _____. (when adverb)

3 I _____ go swimming.   (when adverb)

4 Put pencils _____ and paper _____.

(where adverbs)

Verbs are doing words.

Past tense verbs tell us what people, animals and things did.

To make the past tense, we usually add ed or d to the verb family name.

> This is the past simple tense.

I answered the telephone.
I talked to my friend.

Another way to make the past tense is like this.

I was singing.
He was playing the piano.
The audience were listening.

We use the past progressive tense when:

> This is the past progressive tense.

• an action goes on for some time.

I was walking for a long time.

• when something else happens at the same time.

I was walking to the shops when it started to rain.

Focus

Read the sentences.

Which two words make up the *past progressive verb* in each sentence?

1 The tiger was prowling in the jungle.

2 You were making too much noise!

3 The horses were galloping in the field.

4 I was wondering where you were!

There are two actions in every sentence.
Say which action was going on *for a long time*.

1 She was reading when the telephone rang.

2 We were playing football when I fell over.

3 The cat jumped on my knee when I was drinking my tea.

4 An owl was hooting when we walked in the woods.

Extension

The **order of the words** changes when we use the **past progressive** in questions.

You were cheering for your team.

Were you cheering for your team?

I was eating my sandwich.

Were you eating your sandwich?

Change these statements into *questions*.

1 You were looking for your book.

2 I was reading it yesterday.

3 They were writing a story.

4 It was snowing all night.

Conjunctions

Conjunctions are joining words.

We use them to **join** sentences.

Give me the rubbish. I will take it outside.

Give me the rubbish **and** I will take it outside.

The sky was grey. It didn't rain.

The sky was grey **but** it didn't rain.

Another useful **conjunction** is **or**.

I will have the chocolate biscuit.

I will have the plain biscuit.

I will have the chocolate biscuit **or** the plain biscuit.

Focus

Use *and*, *but* or *or* to join each pair of sentences.

1 One of our players was hurt.
We won the match.

2 I wanted a plum.
There was one left.

3 I might have pizza for tea.
I might have fish.

4 It rained a lot today.
Josh went out to play.

5 I could watch television.
I could read my book.

Copy the sentences. Join each pair with *and*, *but* or *or*.

1 I have a sister.
   I have a brother.

2 Do you like this book?
   Do you like that book?

3 I have to go to bed.
   I am not tired.

4 Should I go out?
   Should I stay in?

Copy the sentences. Join each pair with *but* or *or*.
Change the coloured words to a pronoun.

1 Did Dan eat all the pizza?
   Did Dan go out for tea?

2 The tiger roared at the hunters.
   The tiger did not attack.

3 The girls can go to the park.
   The girls can go swimming.

Confusing words

It is easy to mix up the words **two**, **too** and **to**.
Two is a **number**.

In **two** days it will be my birthday.

Too can mean **as well**.   **Too** can mean **very**.

You can come, **too**.   These books are **too** heavy!

We use **to** like this.

I am going **to** the park.   **to** eat

Focus

Say – *two, too* or *to*?

1 Please get _____ pencils for me.

2 It is _____ far to walk to the shops!

3 I would like an ice-lolly, _____.

4 It is _____ wet to go out.

5 I have _____ letters to post.

6 If we go to the shops, my sister wants to come, _____.

Copy the sentences.
Fill each gap with *too* or *to*.

1 I want _____ play the piano.

2 I would like to play the piano, _____.

3 Do you think it is hard _____ learn?

4 You can learn if you really want _____.

5 I would like to play the trumpet, _____.

A Copy the sentences.

Fill the gaps with *two*, *too* or *to*.

1 The _____ times table is easy.

2 I am going _____ a party today.

3 I am _____ tired _____ stay up late.

4 If you get _____ many spellings wrong, you will have _____ learn them again.

5 I made _____ mistakes.

B This sentence uses the words *two*, *too* and *to*.

The *two* dogs ran *to* the tree but it was *too* hard *to* climb.

Make up your own sentence using *two*, *too* and *to*.

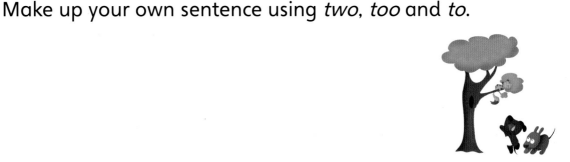

Conjunctions

Conjunctions are words we use to join sentences.

The **conjunctions and**, **but** and **or** are used to join sentences.

I like chocolate cake **and** I ate a big slice.

I like chocolate cake **but** I was too full to eat any.

I sometimes like chocolate cake **or** I sometimes like fruit.

Two other useful conjunctions are **so** and **because**.

Put the chairs on the table.
I can sweep the floor.
Put the chairs on the table **so** I can sweep the floor.

I don't eat liver.
I don't like it.
I don't eat liver **because** I don't like it.

Focus

Say *so* or *because* to join each pair of sentences.

1 Take a coat. It might rain later.

2 I climbed the tree. I could see over the roof.

3 The lion prowled around. It was hungry.

4 Close the gate. The dog will not get out.

5 I want to go home. It is time to eat.

Copy and join each pair of sentences.
Change the coloured words into *pronouns*.

1 My brother and I woke up early.
My brother and I heard the birds singing.

2 Liam lost his key.
Liam could not unlock the door.

3 The football fans cheered.
The football fans saw their
team score a goal.

Extension

We can also join sentences with when, if and that.

I read a book when I was bored.
I wear gloves if it is cold.
This is the hamster that escaped.

Copy and join each pair of sentences
using *when*, *if* or *that*.

You can only use
each one once.

1 We went to bed. It was dark outside.

2 I like parties. There are lots of biscuits.

3 Ella went to the shop. It was closed.

Adverbs

Adverbs tell us more about **how**, **when** or **where** something is done.

How?	Sam clapped loudly.
When?	Mandy fell off her bike yesterday.
Where?	I put the flowers outside.

Adverbs can describe the **difference between two actions**.

hard   +   er   =   hard**er**

He works hard.   He worked hard**er**.

 These are **comparative** adverbs.

Adverbs can describe the **difference between more than two actions**.

He works hard.
He worked harder.
He works the hard**est**.

These are **superlative** adverbs.

Focus

Say the *comparative* and *superlative* adverbs.

1 He arrived late.   He arrived _____.   He arrived the ____.

2 She ran fast.   She ran _____.   She ran the _____.

3 It jumped high.   It jumped _____.   It jumped the _____.

4 I was near.   I was _____.   I was the _____.

5 We tried hard.   We tried _____.   We tried the _____.

Copy the sentences.
Fill each gap with an *adverb* from the box.

| nearer | hardest | highest | faster |

1 He kicked the ball the _____ of all the team.

2 I can run _____ than you.

3 She lives _____ to the school than her friend.

4 That bird is flying the _____.

Write these headings.

| adverb | comparative adverb | superlative adverb |

Write each word in the box under the correct heading.

later	faster	nearer	harder	highest
hardest	high	near	late	higher	nearest
fast	latest	fastest	hard

Nouns

A **noun** is a naming word.   book   cat

An **adjective** is a describing word.   old book   black cat

A **suffix** can be added to an **adjective** to make a **noun**.

<u>adjective</u>   <u>noun</u>

dark   +   ness   =   the dark**ness**

A **suffix** can be added to a **verb** to make a **noun**.

<u>verb</u>				<u>noun</u>
paint	+	er	=	the paint**er**
paint	+	ing	=	the paint**ing**

A **suffix** is added to the end of a word.

Some **nouns** are made from **verbs**.

I **manage** the hotel.   manage = **verb**

I am the **manager**.   manage**r** = **noun**

Focus

Add the *suffix ness* to the adjective. Say the *noun*.

<u>adjective</u>   <u>noun</u>

1 weak   +   ness   =   _____

2 cool   +   ness   =   _____

3 kind   +   ness   =   _____

4 sad   +   ness   =   _____

5 dry   +   ness   =   _____

Add the *suffixes er* and *ing* to the verb. Say the nouns.

verb				noun
1 to swim	+	er	=	_____
	+	ing	=	_____
2 to sing	+	er	=	_____
	+	ing	=	_____
3 to travel	+	er	=	_____
	+	ing	=	_____

Copy the sentences. Make the *nouns* by adding *ness*, *er* or *ing* to the word in brackets.

1 The (dim) of the light made it difficult to read.

2 The (walk) was very fit.

3 The (windsurf) was great fun.

4 The (bright) of the sun hurt my eyes.

5 My (swim) is getting better.

Adjectives

Adjectives are describing words.
They describe **nouns**.

a **tall** tower

a **frightened** rabbit

We can add the suffix **ful** to words to make interesting **adjectives**.

a **colourful** rainbow

a **painful** thumb

We can add the suffix **less** to words to make interesting **adjectives**.

a **helpless** bird

a **harmless** insect

Focus

Do the word sums. Say the *adjectives*.

1 truth   +   ful   = _____   **2** peace + ful   = _____

3 play   +   ful   = _____   **4** help   + ful   = _____

5 home   +   less   = _____   **6** end   + less   = _____

7 worth   +   less   = _____   **8** fear   + less   = _____

A Solve the clues with *ful* or *less* adjectives.

1 If you do not tell lies, you are   <u>truth   </u>.
2 If something seems to go on forever, it is   <u>end   </u>.
3 If you have nowhere to live, you are   <u>home   </u>.
4 If something has no value, it is   <u>price   </u>.
5 If it is quiet and calm, it is   <u>peace   </u>.

B Add an *adjective* from the box to each noun.

colourless	priceless	boastful	faithful

1 a _____ jewel   2 a _____ liquid

3 a _____ winner   4 a _____ dog

Add *full* or *less* to the words in the box.
Use the *adjectives* to complete the sentences.

care	cheer	use	success

1 He ran well and was _____.

2 The teapot was broken and _____.

3 The _____ boy broke the window with his football.

4 She is always smiling and _____.

How to use this book

The heading tells you what the grammar topic is.

The information box tells you about the grammar topic.

The owl gives you extra information.

UNIT 19 Verbs

Verbs are doing words.
Past tense verbs tell us what people, animals and things did.
To make the past tense, we usually add ed or d to the verb family name.

This is the past simple tense.

I combed my hair.   I washed my face.
I walked to the door.   I picked up my bag.

Another way to make the past tense is like this:

This is the past progressive tense.

Past tense of the verb to be		+ verb family name	+ ing	
I	was	sing	ing	I was singing.
You	were	point	ing	You were pointing.
He	was	help	ing	He was helping.
She	was	laugh	ing	She was laughing.
It	was	rain	ing	It was raining.
We	were	jump	ing	We were jumping.
You	were	shout	ing	You were shouting.
They	were	fight	ing	They were fighting.

Focus

Read the sentences.
Which two words make up the *past progressive tense*?
1 The birds were flying around the garden.
2 The tree was bending in the wind.
3 The ducks were quacking for some food.
4 The dog was scattering leaves everywhere.

42

Practice

These sentences are in the present tense.
Change the underlined verb to the *past tense*.

1 I <u>am playing</u> with my dog.

2 You <u>are watching</u> television.

3 He <u>is reading</u> a book.

4 She <u>is washing</u> her hair.

5 It <u>is raining</u>.

6 We <u>are going</u> on holiday.

7 They <u>are visiting</u> the castle.

Each verb is made up of two words.

Extension

Copy and complete these sentences with *past tense verbs*.

1 I _____ _____ a snowman.

2 We _____ _____ when we saw the accident.

3 She _____ _____ to bed very late.

4 He _____ _____ breakfast when the post came.

43

You might want to discuss these questions with a talk partner before answering them.

The tips box tells you more about answering the question.

Sometimes your teacher might ask you to fill in Activity Sheets.

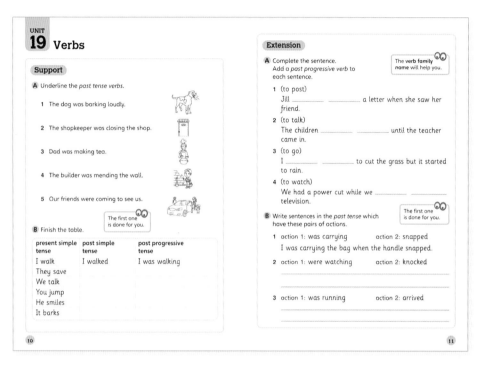

Support

A Underline the *past tense verbs*.

1 The dog was barking loudly.

2 The shopkeeper was closing the shop.

3 Dad was making tea.

4 The builder was mending the wall.

5 Our friends were coming to see us.

The first one is done for you.

B Finish the table.

present simple tense	past simple tense	past progressive tense
I walk	I walked	I was walking
They save		
We talk		
You jump		
He smiles		
It barks		

10

Extension

A Complete the sentence. Add a *past progressive verb* to each sentence.

The verb family name will help you.

1 (to post)
Jill _____ _____ a letter when she saw her friend.

2 (to talk)
The children _____ _____ until the teacher came in.

3 (to go)
I _____ _____ to cut the grass but it started to rain.

4 (to watch)
We had a power cut while we _____ _____ television.

B Write sentences in the *past tense* which have these pairs of actions.

The first one is done for you.

1 action 1: was carrying   action 2: snapped
I was carrying the bag when the handle snapped.

2 action 1: were watching   action 2: knocked
_____
_____

3 action 1: was running   action 2: arrived
_____
_____

11

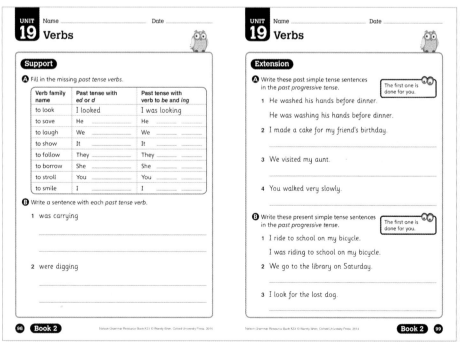

Support

A Fill in the missing *past tense verbs*.

Verb family name	Past tense with ed or d	Past tense with verb to be and ing
to look	I looked	I was looking
to save	He _____	He _____
to laugh	We _____	We _____
to show	It _____	It _____
to follow	They _____	They _____
to borrow	She _____	She _____
to stroll	You _____	You _____
to smile	I _____	I _____

B Write a sentence with each *past tense verb*.

1 was carrying
_____
_____

2 were digging
_____
_____
_____

Nelson Grammar Resource Book KS1 © Wendy Wren, Oxford University Press 2014

Extension

A Write these past simple tense sentences in the *past progressive tense*.

The first one is done for you.

1 He washed his hands before dinner.
He was washing his hands before dinner.

2 I made a cake for my friend's birthday.
_____

3 We visited my aunt.
_____

4 You walked very slowly.
_____

B Write these present simple tense sentences in the *past progressive tense*.

The first one is done for you.

1 I ride to school on my bicycle.
I was riding to school on my bicycle.

2 We go to the library on Saturday.
_____

3 I look for the lost dog.
_____

Nelson Grammar Resource Book KS1 © Wendy Wren, Oxford University Press 2014